W9-AMK-827

LITTLE KIDS
FIRST
BiG
BOOK

ROCKS, MINERALS, AND SHELLS

Moira Rose Donohue

NATIONAL GEOGRAPHIC KIDS

WASHINGTON, D.C.

Contents

Introduction

This book introduces readers to the fascinating world of rocks, minerals, and shells. It answers questions from "What are rocks and minerals?" and "How did they form?" to "Why does the animal inside an oyster shell make a pearl?" The first chapter introduces the topic of rocks, minerals, and shells. The next two chapters feature examples of both common and unusual rocks and minerals, and the last chapter highlights a selection of shells from around the world. Incorporating games and activities, this book teaches young children how to identify a wide range of rocks, minerals, and shells.

Chapter One begins the book by explaining what makes a rock a rock and a shell a shell. Readers learn that most rocks are made of one or more minerals, and that most seashells are the hard outer skeletons of animals called mollusks.

Chapter Two introduces a wide range of rocks, from granite to sandstone to slate. It looks at how these rocks are formed and how they ultimately appear on Earth's surface. A game at the end of this chapter features a map showing where some magnificent natural rock formations—such as El Capitan and Giant's Causeway—are found, as well as where some famous buildings and statues made from rock are located.

Chapter Three explores the vast world of minerals. It discusses the properties of specific minerals and how they were formed, as well as the common uses of some minerals. Minerals that become vibrant gemstones when polished are also included. A fun game wraps up this chapter.

Chapter Four introduces a variety of beautiful seashells that young readers might find on the beach. It also describes the mollusks that live in these shells, including univalves, bivalves, and more. It explains how these animals eat and move, and reveals qualities about some very special mollusks, such as the geography cone snail, which can swallow an entire fish. This chapter ends with a map game featuring several of these creatures.

How to Use This Book

photographs illustrate each [su]pporting the text. Galleries [show] the remarkable diversity of [mi]nerals, and shells.

Fact boxes give the young reader a quick overview of each featured rock or mineral, including color, texture, and hardness. Fact boxes for shells include color, size, and the type of mollusk that lived inside each shell, as well as where the shell is usually found.

Basalt

This dark gray rock was once red-hot!

Magma, the hot liquid rock inside Earth, sometimes erupts from a volcano. These volcanic eruptions can happen either on land or underwater.

Once the magma reaches Earth's surface, it's called lava. When some types of lava flow out of a volcano and cool quickly, they harden into basalt.

Sometimes basalt lava forms in ripples, like this. Then it's called pahoehoe (PUH-ho-ee-ho-ee) basalt.

FACTS

BASALT (buh-SALT)

TYPE igneous

COLOR dark gray to black

TEXTURE fine

One way to identify a rock is by its texture, or how it feels—smooth, fine (gritty), medium, coarse (rough), or porous (filled with holes).

ROCK STARS

GIANT'S CAUSEWAY

Thousands of basalt columns that formed millions of years ago stand at the Giant's Causeway in Northern Ireland. They look like huge sets of stairs built for some very big creatures!

What is the highest staircase you've ever climbed?

20

21

[A]ctive **questions** in each section [encour]age conversation related to the topic.

[Fun] **facts** sprinkled throughout provide [in]formation about the rocks, minerals,

The back of the book offers **parent tips** that include fun activities that relate to rocks, minerals, and shells, along with a helpful **glossary.**

CHAPTER 1
Look Down!

SHELLS AND STONES ON A BEACH IN
CAPE COD, MASSACHUSETTS, U.S.A.

Next time you go outdoors, look down. Maybe you can find a smooth stone. Or you might see a shiny seashell. In this chapter, you will learn what makes a rock a rock and a shell a shell.

Solid Facts About Rocks, Minerals, and Shells

From mountains high above to pebbles at your feet, rocks are everywhere. They can be big or small, shiny or dull, smooth or rough. Most are hard. But a few are soft and can crumble in your hand.

Almost all rocks are made of minerals. Minerals are solid materials found in nature that are not made by plants or animals or other living things. Salt and gold are both minerals. Some rocks are made of only one mineral. Others contain many minerals.

A scientist who studies and identifies rocks is called a geologist.

On the shore near an ocean or a river, you might see shells at your feet. A shell is the hard outer skeleton of snails and sea animals such as clams and oysters. These animals are called mollusks.

A scientist who studies mollusk shells is called a conchologist.

A shell protects the mollusk inside it. When a shell washes up on a shore, it is usually because the mollusk is no longer inside.

Not every animal that has a shell is a mollusk. Turtles have shells, but they are reptiles.

In this book, you'll learn about seashells you might see on a beach near you and shells found on beaches far from your home. You'll explore rocks you might find near your house and rocks that form enormous mountains.

CHAPTER 2

Rock Stars

TEN PEAKS MOUNTAINS, ALBERTA, CANADA

In this chapter, you will discover how rocks form and read about rocks that formed underwater, rocks that float, rocks that were once red-hot liquid, and even rocks from outer space!

Digging In

There are three types of rocks: igneous, sedimentary, and metamorphic. They get their names from how they are formed.

Igneous rocks form from magma, the hot liquid found inside Earth. Sometimes the magma rises up and breaks through the surface. Then it is called lava. When the lava cools down, it hardens into rock.

Devils Tower in Wyoming, U.S.A., is made of igneous rock that formed when magma cooled.

DEVILS TOWER

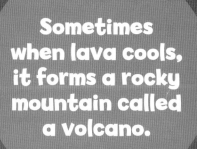

ACATENANGO VOLCANO, GUATEMALA

Sometimes when lava cools, it forms a rocky mountain called a volcano.

Sedimentary rocks form when pieces of rock called sediment break off from other rocks and are carried away by rain and wind. This sediment collects where land dips down, like in valleys and riverbeds. Over time, these broken bits of rock stick together and new rocks are formed.

PEBBLE BEACH AT LAKE SUPERIOR, ONTARIO, CANADA

Earth's surface, or crust, is made up of large slabs of rock called tectonic plates. Sometimes these plates shift and squeeze each other slowly. This movement creates heat and pressure that changes rocks into new rocks, called metamorphic rocks.

Most metamorphic rocks form deep inside Earth. Over time, they are pushed up to the surface where we can see them.

The heat and pressure deep inside Earth can melt rocks. A scientist looks at this melted rock, or lava, inside the top of a volcano.

THE ROCK CYCLE

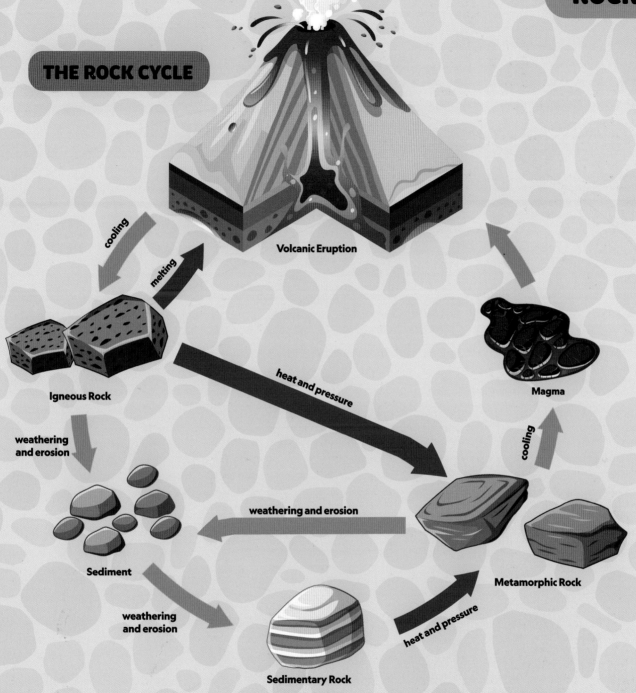

Rocks are always changing. For example, wind and water break rocks into smaller pieces. The pieces get pressed together to form new rock. It can take thousands of years for one rock to change into another. Scientists call this process the rock cycle.

Basalt

This dark gray rock was once red-hot!

Magma, the hot liquid rock inside Earth, sometimes erupts from a volcano. These volcanic eruptions can happen either on land or underwater.

Once the magma reaches Earth's surface, it's called lava. When some types of lava flow out of a volcano and cool quickly, they harden into basalt.

FACTS

BASALT
(buh-SALT)

TYPE
igneous

COLOR
dark gray to black

TEXTURE
fine

One way to identify a rock is by its texture, or how it feels—smooth, fine (gritty), medium, coarse (rough), or porous (filled with holes).

Sometimes basalt lava forms in ripples, like this. Then it's called pahoehoe (PUH-ho-ee-ho-ee) basalt.

GIANT'S CAUSEWAY

Thousands of basalt columns that formed millions of years ago stand at the Giant's Causeway in Northern Ireland. They look like huge sets of stairs built for some very big creatures!

What is the highest staircase you've ever climbed?

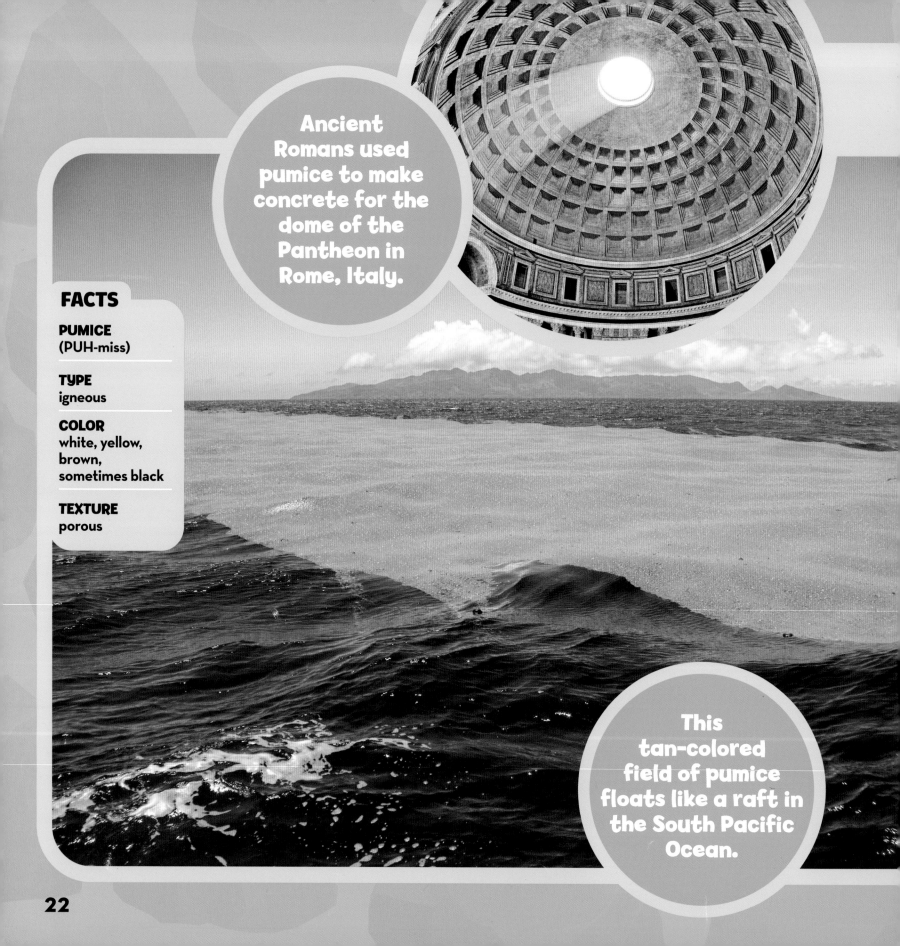

Ancient Romans used pumice to make concrete for the dome of the Pantheon in Rome, Italy.

FACTS

PUMICE
(PUH-miss)

TYPE
igneous

COLOR
white, yellow, brown, sometimes black

TEXTURE
porous

This tan-colored field of pumice floats like a raft in the South Pacific Ocean.

Pumice
This rock is so light, it floats!

Have you ever shaken a can of soda? When you pop it open, foam spurts out. Sometimes volcanoes explode so quickly that lava fills up with gas bubbles, like fizzy soda. When the frothy lava cools and hardens, the rock that forms is full of holes. This rock is called pumice.

MOUNT ST. HELENS

When Mount St. Helens in Washington State, U.S.A., erupted in 1980, it left behind fields of pumice on the ground. Pumice also floats in water because it has so much gas trapped inside. An underwater volcano near the Tonga Islands in the South Pacific created a field of floating pumice.

Have you ever floated on the water? Did you use anything to help you float?

Granite

This rock-star rock is found on all the continents.

Granite develops when magma slowly cools underground. The magma hardens into a rock before it ever comes to the surface. Minerals like quartz form large crystals inside the rock.

FACTS

**GRANITE
(GRAN-it)**

TYPE
igneous

COLOR
white, light gray, pink, red

TEXTURE
coarse

An ancient Egyptian monument, the Lateran Obelisk now stands in Rome, Italy. It is made of red granite from Egypt.

MOUNT KATAHDIN, MAINE, U.S.A.

Over millions of years, rain and wind wear away the rocks and soil on Earth's surface. Then the granite underneath is uncovered.

Sometimes pressure or movement deep inside Earth can push granite to the surface. The soaring granite rock formation of El Capitan at Yosemite National Park in California, U.S.A., formed underground. About 10 million years ago, a shift in Earth's tectonic plates forced the rocks upward. Tall mountains like Mount Katahdin in Maine, U.S.A., are made of granite, too.

EL CAPITAN

Granite was used to make part of the Great Wall of China.

Granite is one of the hardest rocks in the world. It can be used to build huge structures, such as Brihadeeswarar Temple in India, or it can be polished and used for smaller things, like kitchen countertops.

Granite sometimes forms in a large structure called a batholith.

A BATHOLITH IN IDAHO, U.S.A.

BRIHADEESWARAR TEMPLE

Tuff

This rock is not as tough as its name!

Boom! Some volcano eruptions are like big explosions. Hot ashes, pieces of rock, and lava burst into the air. When this volcanic material falls down to the ground, it sometimes sticks together and forms rock. This rock is called tuff. Tuff is often found around a volcano's vent, or opening.

FACTS

TUFF

TYPE
igneous

COLOR
light to dark brown or gray

TEXTURE
porous and sometimes layered

These rock formations in Yellowstone National Park, U.S.A., are made of tuff.

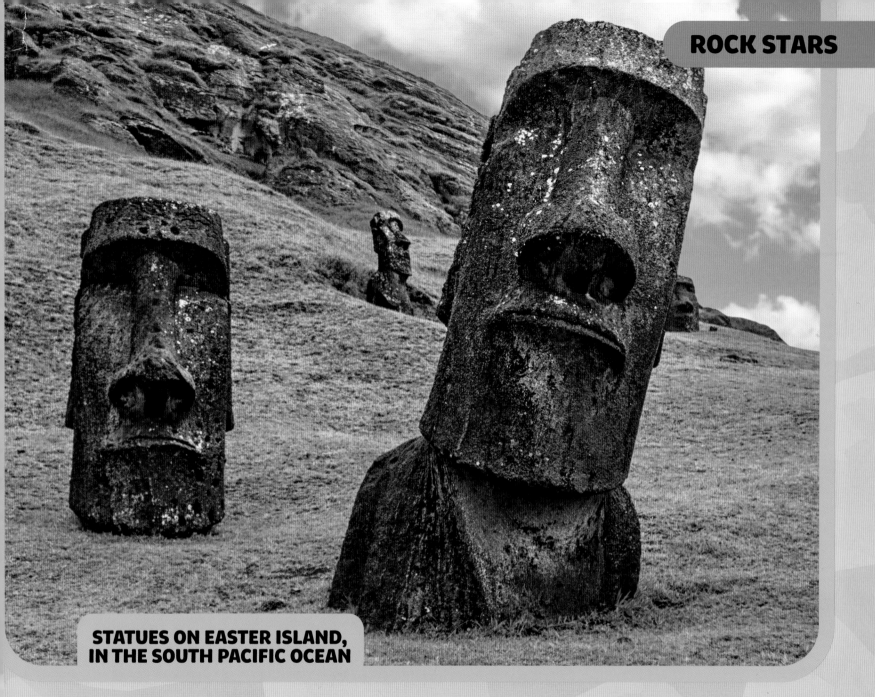

STATUES ON EASTER ISLAND, IN THE SOUTH PACIFIC OCEAN

Tuff is not a very hard rock. Hundreds of years ago, people dug entire villages into the sides of tuff cliffs in northern Italy. On Easter Island, you can see giant human statues carved from tuff.

If you could carve rock, what would you make?

Sandstone

This rock is made of leftovers.

FACTS

SANDSTONE

TYPE
sedimentary

COLOR
many shades of
light brown to red

TEXTURE
fine to coarse

This common sedimentary rock is formed from sand-size grains of minerals and other rocks that have broken down over time. Water and wind carry these small pieces of sediment to many places around the world. Some tiny pieces end up in low-lying areas, like the bottoms of lakes and streams. Over thousands of years, the water dries up. New minerals form and glue the sediment together to make sandstone.

Formed from sandstone, the Rainbow Mountains in Gansu, China, appear brightest just after it rains.

How many colors do you see in these mountains?

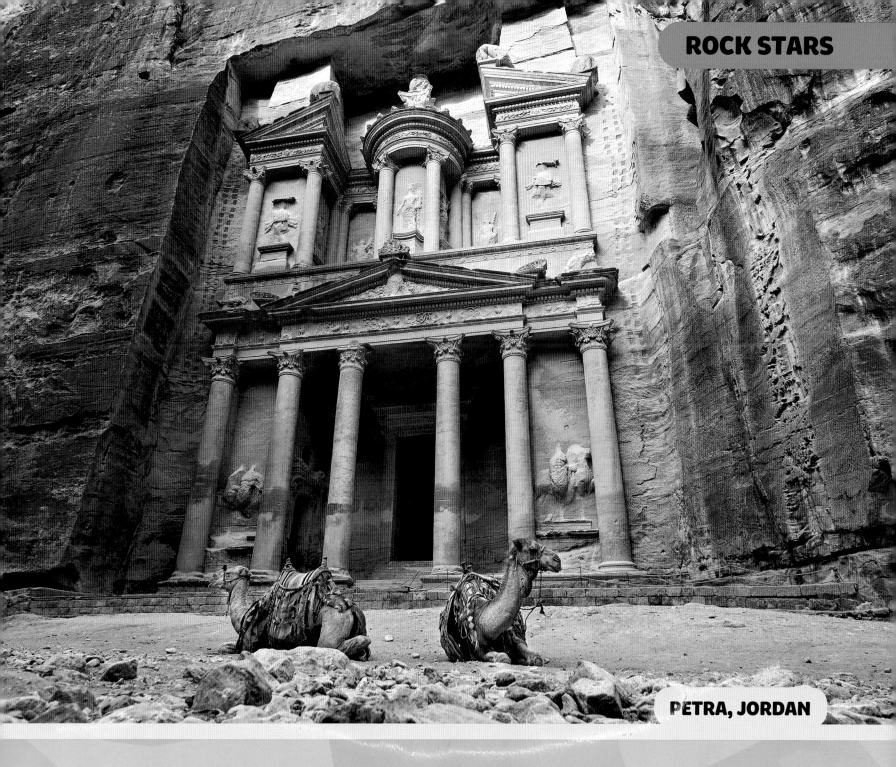

PETRA, JORDAN

More than 2,000 years ago, people who lived in the deserts of Jordan carved caves and temples into pink sandstone cliffs. Later, the ancient Romans added more elaborate buildings. This became the city of Petra. Because of its color, it is also known as the Rose City.

Coal

This rock comes from plants that lived millions of years ago.

Before even dinosaurs existed, Earth was covered with shallow seas and thick forests. The seas sometimes flooded the forests, turning them into swamps. Plants were buried underwater. Over time, these plants piled up at the bottom of swamps. They were buried by layers of sediment. After millions of years, the plant material was changed into a rock called coal.

FACTS

COAL
(KOHL)

TYPE
sedimentary

COLOR
black

TEXTURE
very fine

Lignite is a type of coal found near Earth's surface.

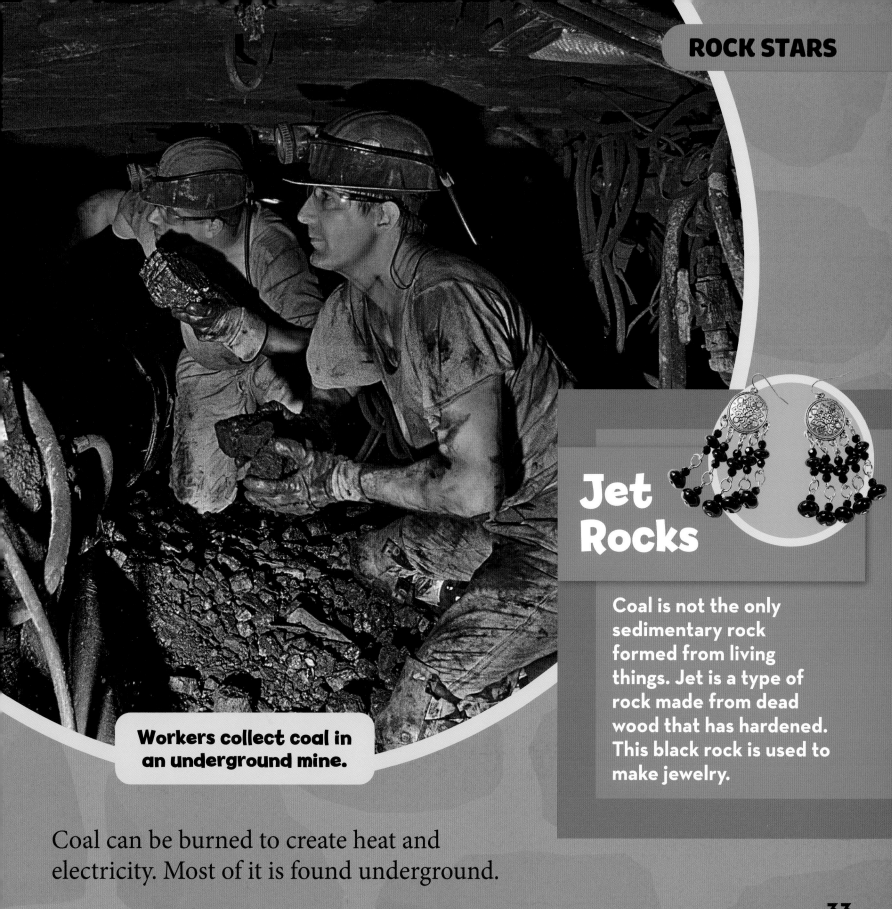

Workers collect coal in an underground mine.

Jet Rocks

Coal is not the only sedimentary rock formed from living things. Jet is a type of rock made from dead wood that has hardened. This black rock is used to make jewelry.

Coal can be burned to create heat and electricity. Most of it is found underground.

FACTS
LIMESTONE

TYPE
sedimentary

COLOR
white, gray, pink

TEXTURE
fine to medium

The Great Sphinx statue in Egypt was carved from limestone. It has the head of a person and the body of a lion.

Limestone
This rock was made from seashells.

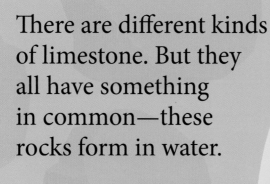

There are different kinds of limestone. But they all have something in common—these rocks form in water.

One kind of limestone forms at the bottom of the ocean. Over time, the water breaks down the old shells of sea creatures like clams and oysters into tiny pieces. These pieces, called lime, settle at the bottom of warm, shallow waters. Over millions of years, layers of lime build up. The pressure from above squeezes them together and forms limestone.

ROCK OF GIBRALTAR, ON THE COAST OF SPAIN

Part of the foundation of the Parthenon in Greece is limestone.

As tectonic plates move and shift, limestone rocks can get pushed higher and higher on Earth. Sometimes they are pushed really high. The peak of Mount Everest, the highest point on Earth, is made of limestone.

MOUNT EVEREST IN THE HIMALAYAN MOUNTAIN RANGE, ASIA

CARLSBAD CAVERNS, NEW MEXICO, U.S.A.

Another type of limestone forms inside caves. Water drips down from the top of the cave. Minerals are left behind on the cave's ceiling. They slowly form icicle-shaped, rocky columns called stalactites. If the water trickles all the way to the floor of the cave, the minerals slowly pile up. These pillars are called stalagmites.

Would you like to explore a cave? Why?

Chalk

This stone can draw a picture.

Chalk is a form of limestone. It is made up of the hard remains of tiny ancient sea life.

Wind and water erosion and shifting tectonic plates lift chalk from seabeds up to Earth's surface. That's why chalk is found in rocky bluffs, or cliffs, at the edge of the sea. The beautiful White Cliffs of Dover in England are made of chalk.

WHITE CLIFFS OF DOVER

38

FACTS

CHALK

TYPE
sedimentary

COLOR
white or light gray

TEXTURE
very fine

Monument Rocks in Kansas, U.S.A., are mostly chalk. They contain a lot of fossils from ancient sea creatures.

Because chalk is soft, it can be used to write with. Ancient cave art was sometimes drawn with chalk. But the sidewalk chalk you draw with today is made in factories from a different material.

Gymnasts use powdered chalk to keep their hands from slipping off bars.

39

FACTS

SLATE

TYPE
metamorphic

COLOR
usually light to
dark gray

TEXTURE
fine

The heat
and pressure deep
inside Earth can
change slate into
another metamorphic
rock called
schist.

SCHIST

Say my
name:
SHIST

40

Slate
This rock can be wiped clean!

Slate starts out as a sedimentary rock called shale. Over many thousands of years, the heat and pressure deep inside Earth change shale into a different rock—slate.

Slate is harder than shale. It forms in layers. The layers can be separated into thin, flat sheets.

Classroom teachers used to write with chalk on large slate boards, called blackboards. The writing could be erased, so the boards could be used over and over again. Today slate is still used for roof and floor tiles.

What do you like to do over and over again?

Marble

This rock-solid rock used to be limestone.

FACTS

MARBLE

TYPE
metamorphic

COLOR
white, but also comes in red, pink, green, and black

TEXTURE
medium

Marble forms when high heat and pressure changes limestone that has been buried underground. Over millions of years, the limestone becomes a glossy rock that often forms in thick layers.

Marble sometimes has lines running through it. These lines are called veins. They form when different types of minerals are trapped in the limestone. But the purest marble is so white it almost glows.

"DAVID" STATUE

It took
21 years and
20,000 workers
to build the
Taj Mahal.

TAJ MAHAL

Many famous statues and buildings are carved out of marble.
Michelangelo's "David" statue in Florence, Italy, is marble.
The beautiful Taj Mahal in Agra, India, is also made of marble.

A Rock Hound's Gallery

Some people like to collect rocks. Here are some interesting rocks you could put in a collection.

BRECCIA (SEDIMENTARY)

DUNITE (IGNEOUS)

SILTSTONE (SEDIMENTARY)

FOLDED GNEISS (METAMORPHIC)

CONGLOMERATE (SEDIMENTARY)

MICA SCHIST (METAMORPHIC)

OBSIDIAN (IGNEOUS)

Meteorite

This rock is out of this world!

FACTS

METEORITE
(MEE-tee-ur-ite)

TYPE
stony, iron, and
stony-iron

COLOR
black, gray, brown

TEXTURE
varied, but
usually smooth
and full of holes

The oldest rocks on Earth are not from Earth at all! They are meteorites from outer space. Meteorites can come from broken pieces of comets—space snowballs made of frozen gas, rock, and dust that orbit, or go around, the sun.

Meteorites can also come from bits of asteroids, which are large rocks that travel through space. Scientists think a few meteorites came from the moon and Mars.

The Hoba meteorite in Namibia, Africa, is the largest meteorite ever found.

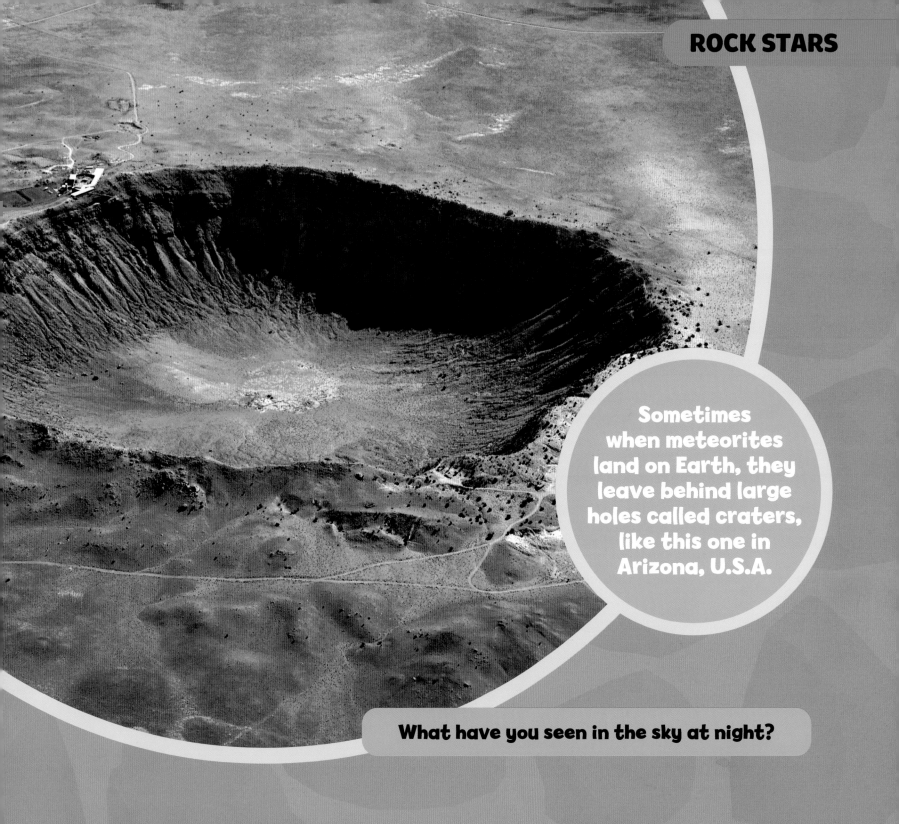

Sometimes when meteorites land on Earth, they leave behind large holes called craters, like this one in Arizona, U.S.A.

What have you seen in the sky at night?

Meteorites fall through Earth's atmosphere. Sometimes they make a streak of light that you can see on a clear night.

Fossils

Fossils can be billions of years older than dinosaurs!

Fossils are the remains of living things—including shells, bones, teeth, and other parts—that have been preserved in rocks. Bones, for example, become buried under sand, mud, and other types of sediment. Sometimes minerals from the watery mud seep into tiny holes in the bones. Over time, the sediment hardens into a rock. The bones harden in the sediment, too, creating a fossil.

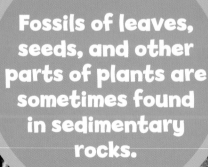

Fossils of leaves, seeds, and other parts of plants are sometimes found in sedimentary rocks.

The oldest dinosaur fossil ever found is about 231 million years old.

Fossils can be found in some sedimentary rocks, such as limestone, shale, and sandstone. Scientists study fossils to learn about dinosaurs and other animals and plants that lived millions of years ago.

FOSSIL

49

Map Fun!

This map shows where many of the amazing statues, buildings, and rock formations you read about in Chapter Two are located. With your finger, draw a line from each clue to the place it describes.

A. **Basalt columns that look like huge steps**

B. **A giant granite rock formation**

C. **Human figures carved from tuff**

D. **A limestone statue with a person's head and a lion's body**

E. **A famous white marble building**

F. **The largest meteorite on Earth**

G. **An ancient city carved into sandstone cliffs**

NORTH AMERICA

EL CAPITAN   United States

ATLANTIC OCEAN

PACIFIC OCEAN

SOUTH AMERICA

EASTER ISLAND STATUES   Easter Island (Chile)

ARCTIC OCEAN

Northern
Ireland
(United Kingdom)

**GIANT'S
CAUSEWAY**

EUROPE

ASIA

**GREAT
SPHINX**

Jordan

PETRA

Egypt

**TAJ
MAHAL**

India

AFRICA

PACIFIC
OCEAN

INDIAN
OCEAN

**HOBA
METEORITE**

Namibia

AUSTRALIA

ANTARCTICA

ANSWERS: A. Giant's Causeway, B. El Capitan,
C. Easter Island statues, D. Great Sphinx,
E. Taj Mahal, F. Hoba meteorite, G. Petra

CHAPTER 3

The Magic of Minerals

MINERAL SALT MINES, CUSCO, PERU

There are more than 5,000 types of minerals on Earth. Each one is different. In this chapter, you will learn about some common—and some unusual—minerals.

Crystal Clear

Most rocks are made up of one or more minerals. Minerals can form in many ways. They can form when water dries up or when magma cools down.

Each mineral forms in its own special shape, called a crystal. Crystals can look like cubes, pyramids, or even columns. Some minerals can be cut and polished to make jewelry. These minerals are called gemstones.

QUARTZ CRYSTALS

How do scientists identify minerals?

Scientists identify minerals by features like crystal shape, hardness (on a scale of 1 to 10, with 10 being the hardest), and luster. Luster can be shiny (metallic), sparkly (brilliant), glassy, pearly, or dull.

This watch is decorated with diamond and ruby gemstones.

Gold

This yellow mineral glistens in the sunlight.

Gold can look like stripes of bright yellow inside rocks. This shiny mineral can also form as large, rounded nuggets deep inside rocks. Over time, wind and water wear away the rock containing the gold. Small bits of these gold nuggets end up in nearby streams and rivers.

FACTS

GOLD

COLOR
rich yellow

HARDNESS
2.5–3

LUSTER
metallic

Have you ever seen gold jewelry?

People rushed to California, U.S.A., when gold was discovered there in 1848. Over several years, they found more than 750,000 pounds (340,000 kg) of gold.

Gold is so heavy that it sinks in water and gets trapped at the bottom of streams. People pan for gold in streams near mountains. They scoop up water and pebbles with a pan that looks like a pie plate. Then they swirl the pan. The water and mud flow over the side. If they are lucky, a little gold flake—or maybe even a nugget—is left behind.

FACTS

PYRITE
(PIE-right)

COLOR
pale to brassy
yellow

HARDNESS
6–6.5

LUSTER
metallic

Pyrite has been
found near the
Rio Tinto mine in Spain,
where people have
also mined copper
for thousands
of years.

RIO TINTO COPPER MINE

Pyrite

This mineral can play tricks.

Pyrite is sometimes called fool's gold. That's because it is yellow and shiny, like gold. But unlike gold, pyrite gets darker when air hits it. And it usually forms eight-sided crystals or perfect six-sided cubes that look like dice.

Gold miners used to bite gold nuggets to see if they were soft, not hard like pyrite.

One big difference between gold and pyrite is that pyrite is hard. You can mold or bend gold with a hammer. But if you hit pyrite, it breaks.

Pyrite gets its name from the Greek word for fire. It gives off a spark when struck or scraped against metals like steel.

Can you name some other cube-shaped things?

Malachite

This mineral is always bright green.

FACTS

MALACHITE
(MAL-uh-kite)

COLOR
green

HARDNESS
3.5–4

LUSTER
brilliant or silky,
sometimes dull

Malachite is often uncovered in caves or caverns that contain the mineral copper. When naturally carbonated, or fizzy, water drips inside the cave and lands on a mineral that has copper in it, a new mineral called malachite forms.

A MALACHITE VASE IN ST. PETERSBURG, RUSSIA

Malachite from the Ural Mountains in Russia was polished and made into beautiful jewelry, boxes, and vases.

Malachite can be ground into a powder to make green paint.

Malachite often looks like a green glob or a bunch of tiny grapes. Sometimes it forms a thin coating on other minerals or is found in small rounded columns. Unlike many minerals, it rarely forms crystals.

Can you spot some things around you that are bright green?

FACTS

DIAMOND

COLOR
usually colorless, but can be yellow, red, pink, blue, green, or black

HARDNESS
10

LUSTER
brilliant

UNCUT DIAMOND

Diamonds are so hard that they can cut through steel!

Diamond

This is the hardest mineral on Earth.

Carbon is a chemical that creates minerals in different forms. One form, called graphite, is very soft. It's used in pencils. Another form is diamond. Most diamonds take millions of years to form. They are created deep inside Earth when there is tremendous heat and pressure.

The largest gem-quality diamond ever found weighed more than 1.37 pounds (621 g). Part of it is now in the British royal scepter.

Diamonds often are found inside a rock called kimberlite. Kimberlite is carried up toward Earth's surface when volcanoes erupt. Over time, kimberlite can get covered up by other rocks. We usually have to dig in mines to find kimberlite with diamonds in it.

Can you find something around you that sparkles?

Gypsum

This mineral may be in the walls all around you.

As water from a sea or salt lake dries up, chemicals in the salty water join together to form crystals. This creates gypsum. Gypsum comes in several varieties. Selenite gypsum is almost clear. It is often found in caves. It can look like giant icicles.

What else looks like an icicle?

FACTS

GYPSUM
(JIP-sum)

COLOR
clear, gray, yellow, pink

HARDNESS
2

LUSTER
glassy, pearly

Sometimes gypsum forms in the shape of a flower. This is called desert rose gypsum.

The Cave of the Crystals in Naica, Chihuahua, Mexico, contains giant stacks of selenite gypsum crystals.

Gypsum looks hard, but it's actually soft. Sculptors often carve a type of gypsum called alabaster into statues. But most gypsum is ground up to make a building material called drywall. The walls inside a lot of houses and schools are made of drywall.

65

Sulfur

This mineral can get stinky!

Sulfur is often found near volcanoes. Pure sulfur appears as bright yellow crystals. The Dallol volcanic crater in Ethiopia is yellow and green because of the sulfur there. The Kawah Ijen volcano in Indonesia has even more sulfur in it. When sulfur gases erupt from the crater, the air makes them burst into blue flames.

FACTS

SULFUR

COLOR
lemon yellow, reddish yellow, brown, gray

HARDNESS
1.5–2.5

LUSTER
greasy

KAWAH IJEN

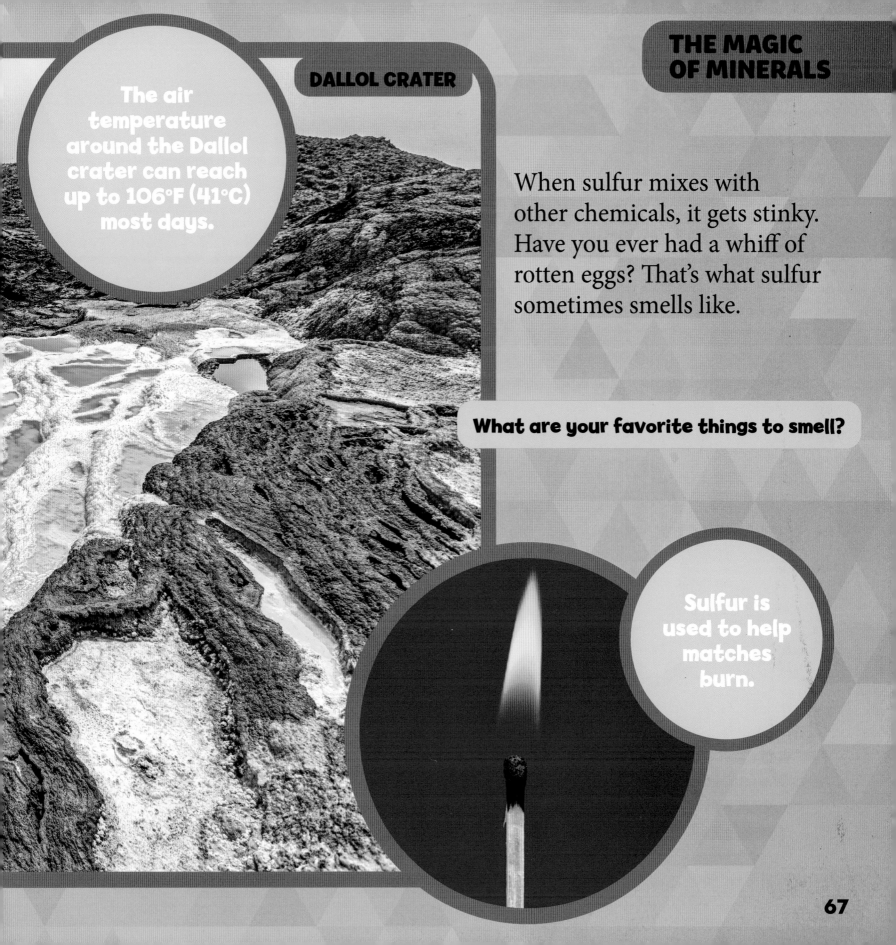

DALLOL CRATER

The air temperature around the Dallol crater can reach up to 106°F (41°C) most days.

When sulfur mixes with other chemicals, it gets stinky. Have you ever had a whiff of rotten eggs? That's what sulfur sometimes smells like.

What are your favorite things to smell?

Sulfur is used to help matches burn.

FACTS

CORUNDUM
(kuh-RUN-dum)

COLOR
white, gray,
brown, red, or
blue

HARDNESS
9

LUSTER
glassy

For centuries, royal families have used rubies and sapphires in jewelry and crowns.

Corundum

This mineral can be a jewel.

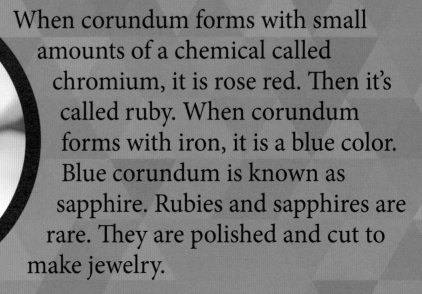

The mineral corundum can be found in all types of rock, but especially in metamorphic rock. Rain and wind slowly break up the rocks into pieces. These little pieces of rock wash into rivers and streams, taking corundum with them.

RUBY RING

When corundum forms with small amounts of a chemical called chromium, it is rose red. Then it's called ruby. When corundum forms with iron, it is a blue color. Blue corundum is known as sapphire. Rubies and sapphires are rare. They are polished and cut to make jewelry.

Which color do you like better—red or blue? Why?

A Jewel Box of Gemstones

Gemstones are rare and beautiful minerals that can be polished and made into jewelry or other objects.

EMERALD-AND-DIAMOND RING

BLACK OPAL RING

SAPPHIRE RING

ONYX-AND-DIAMOND BRACELET

TURQUOISE-AND-DIAMOND CROWN

DIAMOND-AND-EMERALD NECKLACE

RUBY NECKLACE

GOLD-AND-DIAMOND EGG AND CARRIAGE

71

Quartz

If you've built a sandcastle, you might have dug up quartz.

Quartz is one of the most common minerals found on Earth. Tiny quartz crystals glisten in the sand at many beaches. Sand with a lot of quartz in it can be melted. The gooey liquid is then molded into objects. When it cools, you will recognize it as glass.

The largest quartz cluster ever found was in Namibia, Africa.

Sometimes when lightning hits sand, it makes hollow glass tubes in the sand.

Sometimes quartz is harder to find. It hides inside round rocks called geodes. Crack open a geode and you may find quartz crystals inside.

FACTS

QUARTZ
(KWORTZ)

COLOR
usually clear, but comes in various colors

HARDNESS
7

LUSTER
glassy

GEODE

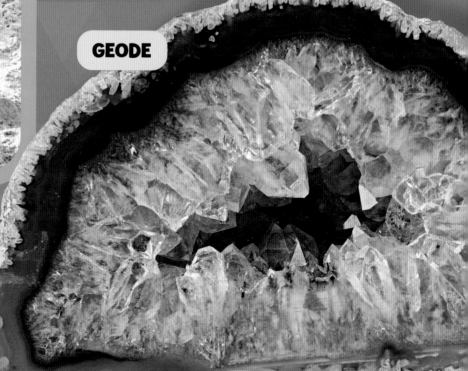

Can you think of another mineral that comes in several colors?
(Hint: See page 68.)

A Rainbow of Quartz

Quartz comes in many different colors. Here are a few.

AMETHYST

SMOKY QUARTZ

PURPLE-AND-YELLOW AMETRINE

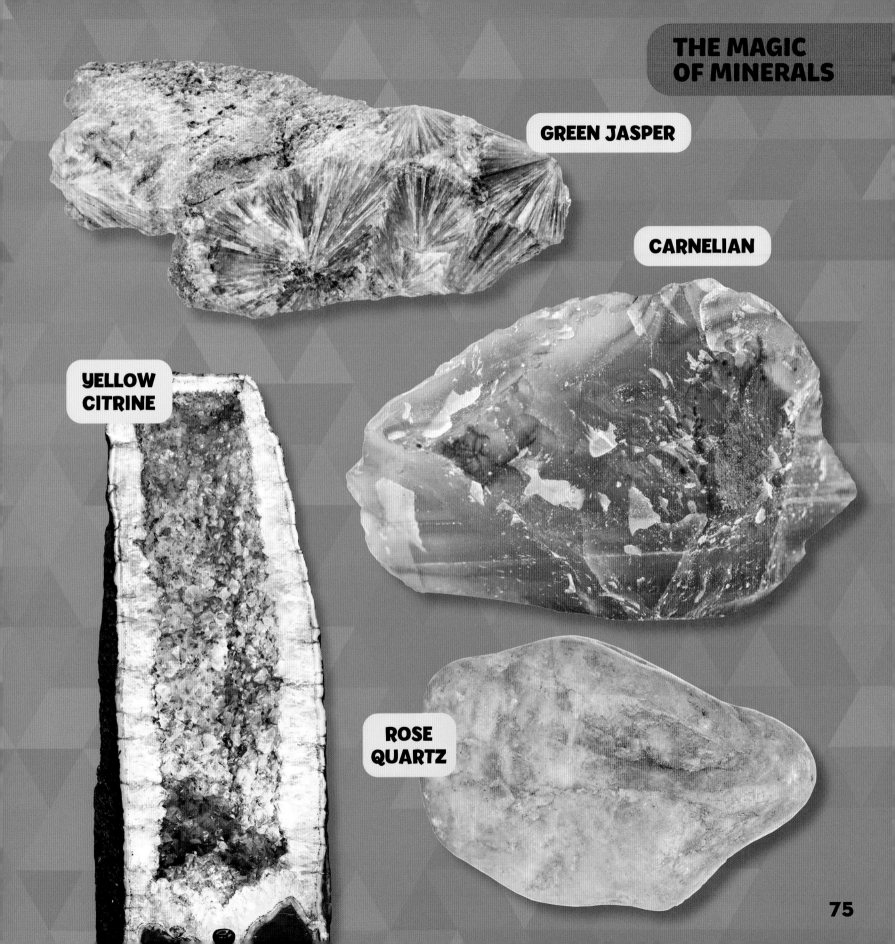

GREEN JASPER

CARNELIAN

YELLOW CITRINE

ROSE QUARTZ

Halite

You can probably find this mineral in your kitchen.

Halite is a mineral that people eat almost every day. It's sprinkled on french fries and popcorn. You know it as salt!

Do you have a favorite salty snack?

FACTS

HALITE

COLOR
clear, gray, yellow, red

HARDNESS
2–2.5

LUSTER
glassy

In the underground salt mines at Wieliczka, Poland, miners carved statues and a church out of salt.

GREAT SALT LAKE

Halite crystals form when salty water evaporates. Large areas of salt, called salt flats, can be seen on the shores of the Great Salt Lake in Utah, U.S.A. Salt flats are also found by the Dead Sea, which lies between the Middle Eastern countries of Jordan and Israel. Some of the salt in your home may have been collected from these natural salt flats.

Salt helps melt ice on streets and sidewalks in the wintertime.

Turquoise

This mineral is the color of the sky on a sunny day.

When water trickles through rock, it sometimes mixes with a metal called copper. The water changes the copper. Then the copper forms a mineral called turquoise.

Sometimes flecks of pyrite (see page 58) get trapped inside turquoise. These flecks make the turquoise sparkle. Other times, tiny bits of nearby rocks get mixed in with the water. They can give turquoise thin brown stripes.

FACTS

TURQUOISE
(TER-kwoiz)

COLOR
sky blue or blue-green

HARDNESS
5-6

LUSTER
waxy, dull

According to Native American legend, when people cried happy tears, their tears became turquoise.

What colors can you see in the sky?

Turquoise is used in the dome of this large mosque in Iran.

Blue minerals are unusual. Ancient Egyptians used this brightly colored mineral in jewelry and art. And it has special meanings to some Native American people in the American Southwest.

FACTS

LABRADORITE

COLOR
clear, white, blue,
iridescent blue

HARDNESS
6–6.5

LUSTER
glassy

This mineral
was discovered in
Labrador, Canada.
That's how it got
its name.

Labradorite

This mineral might remind you of a rainbow.

Labradorite changes color in bright light. It can go from blue to green, then to red, and finally to orange. This is called iridescence.

Labradorite forms in layers with many tiny cracks inside. As light shines through the mineral, the cracks cause the light to bend in different directions. That makes different colors bounce back for your eyes to see.

The iridescent colors in labradorite have been compared to the shimmering colors of the northern lights, which sometimes appear in winter skies in the far north.

Have you ever seen a rainbow? Where?

NORTHERN LIGHTS

81

Autunite

This mineral can sometimes glow brightly.

Under certain light, autunite glows bright green. It contains a chemical called uranium that makes it glow. The uranium also gives off rays of energy, called radiation. That's why the uranium found in autunite can be used to help make electricity in some power plants.

This mineral sometimes forms in the shape of a tiny handheld fan.

FACTS

AUTUNITE
(AW-tuh-nite)

COLOR
lemon yellow to green

HARDNESS
2–2.5

LUSTER
pearly, waxy, fluorescent

Autunite was first discovered near Autun, France. That's how it got its name.

AUTUN, FRANCE

Autunite is found in certain types of granite. It usually forms in a thin layer or crust on top of another mineral.

83

Let's Play a Game!

GARNET

AMETHYST

AQUAMARINE

DIAMOND

EMERALD

ALEXANDRITE

A

B

C

D

E

F

Some minerals look dull and cloudy when found in nature.
After they are cut with tools and polished, they become clear and sparkly.
Called gems, they are often used to make jewelry. With your finger, draw a
line from each gem to how that mineral looks before it is cut and polished.

RUBY

PERIDOT

SAPPHIRE

PINK
TOURMALINE

TOPAZ

BLUE TOPAZ

G

H

I

J

K

L

ANSWERS: A. sapphire, B. ruby, C. blue topaz, D. topaz, E. amethyst, F. pink tourmaline,
G. diamond, H. emerald, I. aquamarine, J. alexandrite, K. peridot, L. garnet

85

CHAPTER 4
Seashell Secrets

SHELLS AND STONES ON CHRISTMAS ISLAND, IN THE INDIAN OCEAN

Stroll along a sandy beach and you're sure to see some shells. In this chapter, you will learn about the animals that lived in them.

A Shell Home

GARDEN SNAIL

As a mollusk grows, its shell grows with it.

If you touch your elbow, you can feel the bone inside your body. That's part of your skeleton. Mollusks are animals that have skeletons on the outside of their body. Their skeletons are called shells. A mollusk's hard shell keeps it safe. The shell is its home.

Mollusks have soft bodies and one large foot. Snails in your garden are mollusks. So are sea animals like clams and oysters.

UNIVALVE

BIVALVE

The two most common types of mollusks are univalves and bivalves. Univalves, like snails, have only one shell. Bivalves, like clams, have both a top and a bottom shell.

Some mollusks live in salt water, like the ocean. Others live in freshwater lakes and rivers.

OCTOPUS

A few types of mollusks, like squid and octopuses, don't have a shell on the outside of their bodies.

Purple Dye Murex

This shell was a favorite of ancient Roman emperors.

This sea snail lives in shallow, warm water. It has a special way to protect itself. This mollusk oozes a liquid that tastes bad to predators. When mixed with air, this substance turns a deep purple color.

FACTS

PURPLE DYE MUREX

TYPE
univalve

COLOR
tan or brown

SIZE
about as long as an adult's pointer finger

WHERE IT'S FOUND
Mediterranean Sea

The shell is often covered in green algae, making it hard to see on the ocean floor.

Ancient people collected this shell. They crushed it and boiled it in giant pots. They stirred the mixture until it turned deep purple. Then they dyed clothing with this rich color.

In ancient Rome, only wealthy people or royalty were allowed to wear the color purple.

It took 250,000 shells to make one ounce (28 g) of purple dye.

Can you spy any purple things around you?

Cowrie

The cowrie sea snail keeps its shell shiny.

When the cowrie comes out of its shell to hunt for food at night, part of its body almost completely covers its shell. This polishes the shell and makes it shine.

GOLDEN COWRIES

Golden cowries are rare. They hide on rocky ledges and in caves in the sea.

FACTS

COWRIE
(COW-ree)

TYPE
univalve

COLOR
white, tan, orange, light brown; usually with darker spots

SIZE
usually about the size of a human thumb, but some can be as long as a spoon

WHERE IT'S FOUND
worldwide

SEASHELL SECRETS

There are more than 200 different kinds of cowries. You may have seen a glossy cowrie shell on the beach. These mollusks live in shallow waters around the world.

MAP COWRIE

ATLANTIC GRAY COWRIES

Female cowries cover their eggs with their foot until the eggs hatch.

Cowrie shells were once used as money.

Can you curl up like a cowrie shell?

Geography Cone Snail

Its shell is pretty but hides a secret weapon.

During the day, the geography cone snail buries itself in the sand. But at night, the snail creeps along the ocean floor to find food.

It sticks out a long tube, called a siphon, to find food. Inside another tube is a pointy tooth, like a needle. The snail finds a fish or other prey. The tooth quickly shoots out on a thread and injects the prey with venom.

There are more than 500 different types of cone snails. They are all venomous.

The venom stuns the prey so that it can't swim away. Then, gulp! The cone snail swallows its meal whole.

FACTS

GEOGRAPHY CONE SNAIL

TYPE
univalve

COLOR
white or cream with brown markings

SIZE
about the size of a smartphone

WHERE IT'S FOUND
Indian and Pacific Oceans

These snails sometimes burrow under the sand or hide in coral reefs.

LIGHTNING WHELK

TYPE
univalve

COLOR
white, brown, beige

SIZE
about as long as a computer tablet

WHERE IT'S FOUND
southeastern North America

Sometimes the whelk uses its rough tongue, or radula, to drill a hole into a clam's shell.

Lightning Whelk

The brown zigzags on this shell look like lightning bolts.

The lightning whelk snacks on clams. This sea snail crams its strong foot between the top and bottom of the clam shell. Then it uses the lip of its own shell to keep the clam open. The whelk pushes a long tube, called a proboscis, inside and slurps up the clam.

The largest lightning whelk ever found was taller than a bowling pin.

FOOT

The female lightning whelk lays eggs in a string of tiny capsules. The string can be nearly three feet (0.9 m) long and hold hundreds of eggs. She buries one end of the string at the bottom of the ocean so that it won't float away.

What other animals lay eggs?

97

Queen Conch

This animal can live for more than 30 years.

The queen conch shell is a beautiful rosy pink color. The snail inside has a strong foot that it uses to jump away from predators like turtles and sharks.

Queen conch snails eat algae and seagrass. They look for food with eyes that sit on top of long, slender tubes called eyestalks. These eyestalks stick up through their shells.

If you hold a queen conch shell to your ear, it will make the noises around you sound louder.

98

The queen conch is also called the pink conch.

FACTS

QUEEN CONCH
(konk)

TYPE
univalve

COLOR
tan with pink lip

SIZE
about as long as a fork, sometimes larger

WHERE IT'S FOUND
Caribbean and nearby waters

A full-grown queen conch can be almost as tall as a medium-size dog. But it can take up to five years for the animal to get that big. It oozes a chemical along its shell opening that makes the shell grow larger as the snail grows inside.

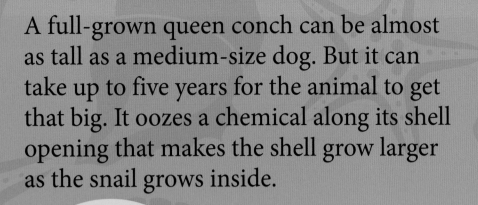

The word *concha* in Spanish means "shell."

For hundreds of years, people have blown through conch shells to call to each other.

What sounds do you hear at the beach?

Here are some other kinds of conchs.

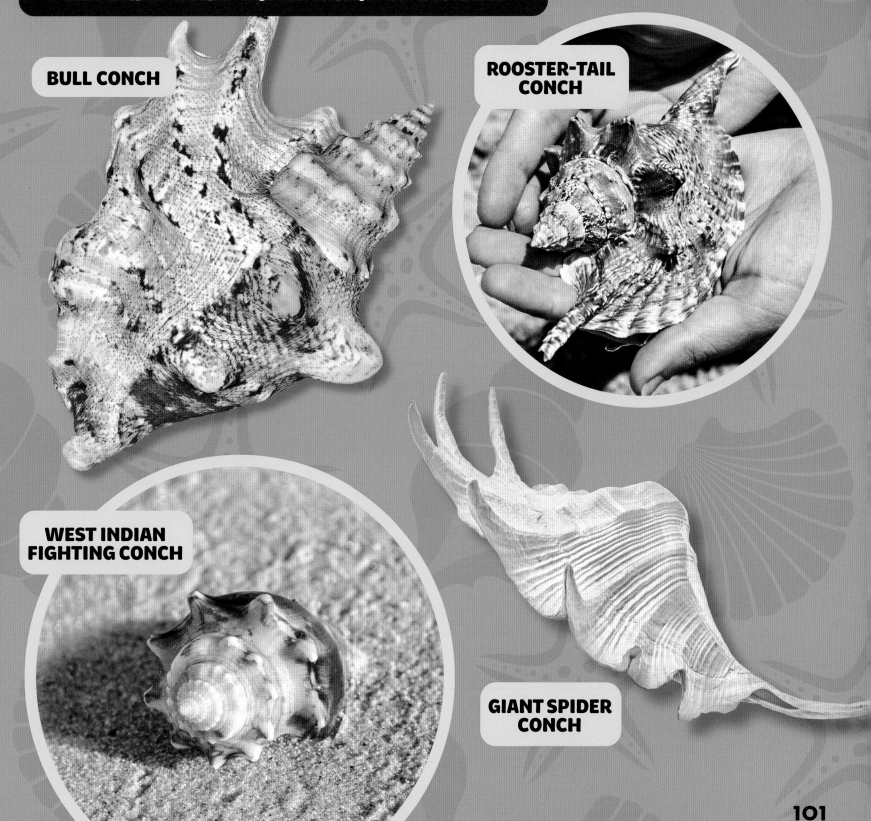

BULL CONCH

ROOSTER-TAIL CONCH

WEST INDIAN FIGHTING CONCH

GIANT SPIDER CONCH

Calico Scallop

This shell has frilly edges.

The calico scallop has bright blue eyes on the rim of its shell. These eyes don't see as well as our eyes do. But they do see changes in light. A shadow in the water might mean a predator is near. Clap, clap! The calico scallop repeatedly slaps its shell open and closed. This pushes water out behind it so that it can swim away.

EYE

TENTACLE

Tentacles on the edge of its shell also help the scallop sense danger.

The scallop is one of the few bivalve mollusks that can move through the water quickly.

What color are your eyes?

The edges of the calico scallop's hinges are called ears.

EARS

CALICO SCALLOP

TYPE
bivalve

COLOR
brown, gold, pink, purple markings

SIZE
about as big as an adult's thumb

WHERE IT'S FOUND
southeastern United States to Brazil

The shape of the scallop shell has been used in art and furniture for centuries.

This scallop's top and bottom shell are held together by a hinge. The mollusk inside opens its shell to suck in water. It filters the water for something tasty to eat, like tiny sea animals called zooplankton.

103

Silver-Lipped Pearl Oyster

This shell can hide a gem inside.

To make its shell stronger, this mollusk makes a substance called nacre (NAY-ker). It coats the inside of its shell with nacre. Sometimes a tiny bit of food or grit gets stuck inside its smooth shell. The grit irritates the mollusk. So it coats that with nacre, too. Over time, the mollusk adds more nacre and a beautiful pearl is formed.

This oyster is the largest of all pearl-making oysters.

FACTS

SILVER-LIPPED PEARL OYSTER

TYPE
bivalve

COLOR
grayish brown

SIZE
between the length of a fork and the length of an adult's foot

WHERE IT'S FOUND
northwest Australia; Indonesia

This oyster's shell feels rough and is a dull gray color on the outside. But on the inside, the shell is smooth and shimmers with many colors.

Almost all bivalve mollusks, including clams and mussels, can make pearls.

Pearls come in different colors. Black-lipped oysters usually make black pearls.

A diver looks at a giant clam shell.

The largest giant clam ever found was 4.5 feet (1.3 m) wide and weighed 550 pounds (249 kg)!

Giant Clam

A giant clam can weigh more than an adult man.

When it's young, a giant clam attaches itself to a rocky tropical reef. It stays there for the rest of its life. And that can be a long time—this clam can live up to 100 years!

What is the biggest animal you can think of?

FACTS

GIANT CLAM

TYPE
bivalve

COLOR
shell is white or gray, but the animal inside can be blue or green

SIZE
about the size of your kitchen stove

WHERE IT'S FOUND
Indian and western Pacific Oceans

A GIANT CLAM IN THE GREAT BARRIER REEF, IN AUSTRALIA

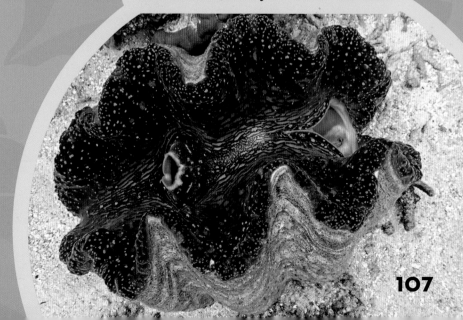

Tiny sea creatures like barnacles often cling to this clam's big shell. Billions of algae live inside its shell. They make food that the giant clam eats. The algae also give the clam its bright green or blue color.

GIANT CLAMS IN THE PHILIPPINES

The giant clam usually keeps its shell open during the day. But if it senses danger, this giant closes up its shell tight.

A GIANT CLAM IN THE GREAT BARRIER REEF

Here are some other kinds of clams.

ANGEL WING CLAM

CHANNELED DUCK CLAM

LAZARUS JEWEL BOX CLAM

RAZOR CLAM

True Heart Cockle

This shell is like a valentine from the sea.

FACTS

TRUE HEART COCKLE

TYPE
bivalve

COLOR
white, yellow, or pink

SIZE
about as long as an adult's thumb

WHERE IT'S FOUND
Indonesia

The cockle is a type of clam. It's usually found in shallow water or burrowed in the sand at the water's edge.

This clam anchors itself to hard surfaces with tiny threads that are made inside its shell.

FLAT SIDE

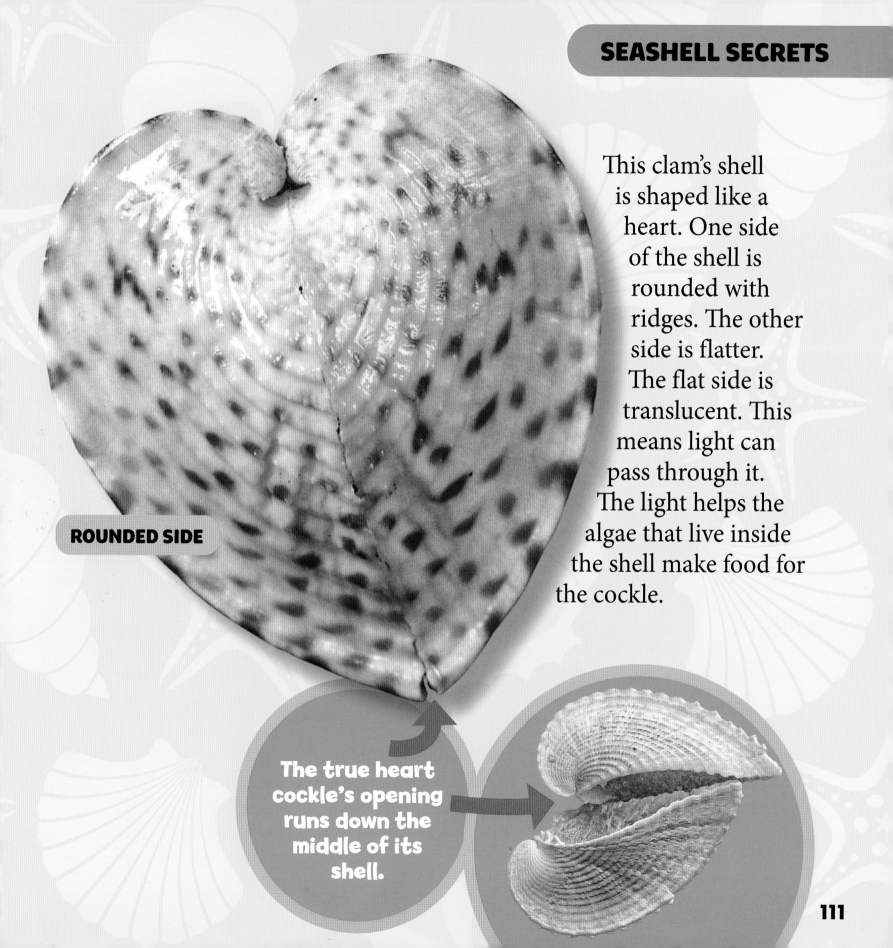

This clam's shell is shaped like a heart. One side of the shell is rounded with ridges. The other side is flatter. The flat side is translucent. This means light can pass through it. The light helps the algae that live inside the shell make food for the cockle.

ROUNDED SIDE

The true heart cockle's opening runs down the middle of its shell.

Chambered Nautilus

This animal is a close relative of squid and octopuses.

The chambered nautilus is a builder. As it grows, it seals off the area it was living in with a layer of shell. Then the nautilus makes a new, bigger chamber, or room. The chambers circle around the shell in a spiral shape. They are connected by tubes.

The nautilus uses the chambers to help it swim. The animal pulls water through a tube and into the empty chambers. Then it pushes the water out. As the water squirts out, the nautilus moves backward.

NAUTILUS FOSSILS

The nautilus has lived on Earth for more than 400 million years.

FACTS

CHAMBERED NAUTILUS
(NAW-tuh-liss)

TYPE
cephalopod

COLOR
creamy with reddish stripes

SIZE
about the size of a teacup; some as large as a dinner plate

WHERE IT'S FOUND
western Pacific Ocean

The nautilus can have up to 90 tentacles. It wraps them around its prey and then pulls the food into its mouth.

How many tentacles can you count on this nautilus?

Tusk Shell

These shells look like elephant tusks.

The animal inside a tusk shell is a scaphopod. It is another type of mollusk.

Its shell is open at both ends. It sticks out its foot through the larger end. It buries its foot in the sand and sends out slender tentacles to search for tiny animals to eat. The tentacles shovel food into its mouth, which is just above its foot.

The mollusk points up the narrow end of its shell to filter water in and out.

FACTS

TUSK SHELL

TYPE
scaphopod

COLOR
white, beige, green, brown

SIZE
about as long as a large paper clip

WHERE IT'S FOUND
in both deep and shallow water everywhere

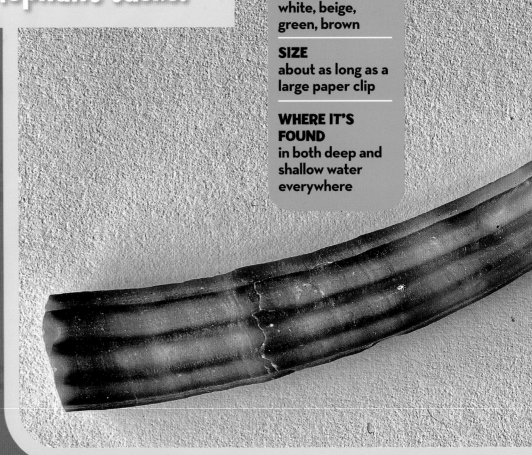

This mollusk spends most of its life with its mouth in the sand.

There are at least 600 kinds of tusk shells. Most are very small.

TUSK SHELLS

Some Native Americans use tusk shells to make jewelry and special clothing for ceremonies.

Shells Galore!

Here are a few more beautiful shells found on beaches around the world.

ABALONE

ATLANTIC FIG

BLUE EDIBLE MUSSEL

SEASHELL SECRETS

COQUINA

LETTERED OLIVE

COMMON LIMPET

BLEEDING TOOTH NERITES

Map Fun!

This map shows where some of the seashells you learned about in this chapter can be found. With your finger, draw a line from the name of the shell to the place where it can be found.

A. Silver-lipped pearl oyster

B. Lightning whelk

C. Queen conch

D. Purple dye murex

E. Geography cone snail

F. Chambered nautilus

G. True heart cockle

NORTH AMERICA

SOUTHEASTERN NORTH AMERICA

CARIBBEAN ISLANDS

ATLANTIC OCEAN

SOUTH AMERICA

WESTERN PACIFIC OCEAN

SEASHELL SECRETS

ARCTIC OCEAN

ASIA

EUROPE

MEDITERRANEAN SEA

PACIFIC OCEAN

AFRICA

INDIAN OCEAN

INDONESIA

NORTHWEST COAST OF AUSTRALIA

AUSTRALIA

ANTARCTICA

ANSWERS: A. northwest coast of Australia, B. southeastern North America, C. Caribbean Sea, D. Mediterranean Sea, E. Indian and Pacific Oceans, F. western Pacific Ocean, G. Indonesia

ROCK ON!

Geologists are scientists who study rocks. They can tell you how, when, and where different kinds of rocks were formed. Here are some items geologists use when they are rock-hunting.

ROCK HAMMER to break off pieces from large rocks, and to crack rocks open to see inside them

GLOVES to protect the hands from sharp pieces of rock

GOGGLES to protect the eyes from flying pieces of rock

BRUSH to clean off dirt from rock samples

MAGNIFYING GLASS to see the tiny minerals inside rocks

BUCKET for carrying samples

NOTEBOOK AND PENCIL to write about the rocks

VINEGAR will fizz on certain minerals, like calcite, and can help identify rocks

WHITE VINEGAR

121

PARENT TIPS

Extend your child's experience beyond the pages of this book. Go for a walk in a park or nature center. Point out large stones and boulders. Let your child pick up small rocks and pebbles. Ask her to compare how they feel. Are they rough or smooth? Do they feel hard or crumbly? What color are they? Look around your house and point out some common places where rocks and minerals are used, like walkways, fireplaces, countertops, and even in your salt shaker. And if you have the chance to go to the seashore, look for seashells and try to identify them with your child. Here are some other activities you can do with National Geographic's *Little Kids First Big Book Rocks, Minerals, and Shells.*

ROCK-STAR ROCK COLLECTOR
(ORGANIZATION/WRITING) Collect small rocks of different colors, hardness, and luster. Wash, dry, and polish them with a cloth. Wipe out an old egg carton. Place one rock in each depression. Using this book and other resources, try to identify each rock. Then, using colored pencils and a piece of paper, help your child write down the names of the rocks in the same order they appear in the egg carton. Cut out and paste the guide to the inside top of the egg carton.

CASTLES IN THE SAND
(MOTOR SKILLS)
The next time your child is at the beach or a sandbox, encourage him to build a sandcastle. Begin by creating a base and pounding it down. Then fill pails or boxes with damp sand to create shapes. Turn them over and dump them onto the base to build a castle. Point out the grains that sparkle. Could they be quartz? Finally, decorate the sandcastle with shells and pebbles.

CRYSTAL SHAPES
(OBSERVATION)
Shake out some table salt onto a piece of black construction paper. Coarse salt or sea salt is best. Then sprinkle some sand onto the black paper. Using a magnifying glass, have your child look at the grains of salt. Are they shaped like cubes or do they have sharp angles? Now look at the sand. Is it the same or are the grains rounded?

BIG ROCK, LITTLE ROCK
(MEASURING)
Pick up 10 or 12 rocks of varying sizes from your yard or neighborhood. Wash and dry them thoroughly. Ask your child to arrange them in order from smallest to largest on a sheet of white paper. Then help your child trace each rock with a pencil. With a ruler, measure the longest part of the outline and write down the number. Are they arranged in size order?

MAKE FOSSILS
(SCIENCE)

Help your child mix 1 cup (275 g) salt, 2 cups (240 g) flour, and 3/4 cup (0.2 L) water until a dough forms. Break off fistfuls, roll into balls, and flatten like round cookies. Then ask your child to press leaves or shells into the rounds of dough. Bake at 200°F (100°C) until dried— usually 45 to 60 minutes (thicker rounds will take longer) or leave them for 24 hours to harden on their own.

ROCKIN' ANIMALS
(ARTS AND CRAFTS)

Find several flat rocks in different sizes. Help your child wash them thoroughly, and then ask her to paint each rock in a different color. When the rocks are dry, stack them up into imaginary animals and glue them together. Add googly eyes and pipe cleaner tails. Or have your child paint faces directly onto the rocks. Be creative!

CLAM UP
(EXERCISE)

Review the section about clams and how they eat and move. Have your child press the palms of his open hands together and rotate them parallel to the ground. Clap hands like a clam would open and close. Then, show your child how to press his arms together and extend them, keeping his hands in the same position. Now clap from the elbow, like a giant clam!

GLOSSARY

MOUNT ETNA, IN ITALY, ERUPTING IN 2013

ALGAE: a group of organisms that usually grow in water, such as kelp and other seaweed

ATMOSPHERE: the mixture of gases that surround a planet

CEPHALOPOD: a mollusk with jaws and arms or tentacles, such as octopus, squid, cuttlefish, and nautilus

CHEMICAL: a physical substance with its own special properties

CRUST: the outermost layer of Earth

CRYSTAL: the shape a mineral takes as it forms in a rock. It often has repeating patterns.

EROSION: the process in which sediment is moved from one place to another

EVAPORATE: to change a liquid into a vapor or gas

GEODE: a hollow, round rock that's often lined with crystals

GEOLOGIST: a scientist who studies rocks

IGNEOUS ROCK: a rock formed by the cooling of superhot liquid rock called magma

IRIDESCENCE: showing the colorful quality of a rainbow

LAVA: melted rock on Earth's surface

MAGMA: hot melted rock that forms inside Earth and comes out as lava

METAMORPHIC ROCK: a rock that has been formed through heating and squeezing or pressure

MINE: a pit or tunnel from which minerals are taken

MINERAL: a natural, nonliving solid substance that forms in a set crystal structure

MOLLUSK: an animal with a soft, unsegmented body like a snail

PLANKTON: tiny plants, algae, and animals that live in water

PREDATOR: an animal that eats other animals (prey)

PRESERVE: to keep or save from decay

PREY: an animal that a predator hunts for food

PROBOSCIS: a long, tubular organ, like a trunk

QUARRY: a place where stone is dug up from the ground

RADULA: a tongue with tiny teeth that helps a mollusk scrape and cut food

SCAPHOPOD: a group of mollusks that have cone-shaped, tusklike shells that are open at both ends

SEDIMENTARY ROCK: a rock that is formed when many small pieces of other rocks are joined together

STALACTITE: an icicle-shaped rock formed by mineral-rich water dripping from the ceiling of a cave

STALAGMITE: a tapering column of rock that forms on the floor of a cave

TECTONIC PLATE: a gigantic piece of Earth's crust that shifts or moves very slowly over time

TRANSLUCENT: describes something that is not completely clear but allows light to pass through

VENOM: a poison that some animals deliver through a bite or a sting

ADDITIONAL RESOURCES

BOOKS

Honovich, Nancy. *Ultimate Explorer Field Guide: Rocks & Minerals.* National Geographic Kids Books, 2016.

Tomecek, Steve, with Carsten Peter. *Everything Rocks and Minerals.* National Geographic Kids Books, 2011.

Tomecek, Steve, illustrated by Nancy Woodman. *Jump Into Science: Dirt.* National Geographic Kids Books, 2016.

Tomecek, Steve, illustrated by Kyle Poling. *Jump Into Science: Rocks and Minerals.* National Geographic Kids Books, 2010.

Tomecek, Steve, illustrated by Fred Harper. *Dirtmeister's Nitty Gritty Planet Earth: All About Rocks, Minerals, Fossils, Earthquakes, Volcanoes & Even Dirt!* National Geographic Kids Books, 2015.

Zoehfeld, Kathleen Weidner. *National Geographic Readers: Rocks and Minerals.* National Geographic Kids Books, 2012.

WEBSITES

Bill Nye Rock Cycle: youtube.com/watch?v=BsIHV_voMk

Minerals and Gems: nationalgeographic.com/science/earth/inside-the-earth/minerals-gems/

Rocks: nationalgeographic.com/science/earth/inside-the-earth/rocks/

GOLD NUGGETS

AMETHYST GEODE

INDEX

PHOTO CREDITS

AS = Adobe Stock; DRMS = Dreamstime; GI = Getty Images; SI = Courtesy of the Smithsonian Institution; SS = Shutterstock

FRONT COVER: (polished gemstones), Tryfonov/AS; (conch shell), Pavel Timofeev/AS; (green vivianite), Albert Russ/SS; (fossil), Mark Brandon/SS; (seashells and pebbles), drasa/SS; (faceted gemstones), J. Palys/SS; (blue topaz), TinaImages/SS; (Yosemite National Park), turtix/SS; SPINE: (amethyst), Sebastian Janicki/SS; BACK COVER: (amethyst), Vinicius Tupinamba/DRMS; (ruby), Zelfit/DRMS; (aquamarine), NickKnight/SS; (rainbow mountains), dinozzaver/AS; (nautilus shell), Danny Iacob/SS; FRONT MATTER: 1, iacomino FRiMAGES/SS; 2-3, Helen Hotson/DRMS; 4, damedias/AS; 5 (UP), JonikFoto.pl/AS; 5 (LO LE), New Africa/AS; 5 (LO RT), Albert Russ/SS; CHAPTER 1: 8-9, JayLazarin/iStock; 10-11, Svetoslav Sokolov/DRMS; 11, simonkr/iStock; 12, Francois Nascimbeni/AFP/GI; 12-13, Diane Kuhl/DRMS; 13, whitcomberd/AS; CHAPTER 2: 14-15, Lubomir Chudoba/DRMS; 16, powerofforever/GI; 16-17, Francoisboudrias/DRMS; 17, Jay Beiler/DRMS; 18, Peter Carsten/National Geographic Image Collection; 19, BlueRingMedia/SS; 20 (UP), siimsepp/AS; 20 (LO), Shane Myers/DRMS; 20-21, Irina Schmidt/AS; 22 (UP), Petunyia/AS; 22 (LO), David Fleetham/Nature Picture Library; 23 (UP), Ekaterina/AS; 23 (LO), World History Archive/Alamy Stock Photo; 24 (UP), vvoe/AS; 24 (LO), Jannis Werner/DRMS; 24-25, Bncc369/DRMS; 26, Yuri Yavnik/SS; 26-27, Yun Gao/DRMS; 27 (LE), Martynelson/DRMS; 27 (RT), Dinodia Photos/Alamy Stock Photo; 28 (UP), sokolenok1/AS; 28 (LO), Jacob W. Frank/NPS Photo/Alamy Stock Photo; 29, ESB Professional/SS; 30 (UP), michal812/AS; 30 (LO), dinozzaver/AS; 31, alekosa/AS; 32 (UP), Shtraus Dmytro/SS; 32 (LO), MichaelDrapeau/iStock; 32-33, Oliver Berg/picture alliance/GI; 33, Malivan_Iuliia/AS; 34, Shtraus Dmytro/SS; 35 (UP), aleks-p/AS; 35 (LO), emperorcosar/AS; 36, tilialucida/AS; 37 (UP), Vixit/SS; 37 (LO), douglas knight/SS; 38 (UP), Ekaterina/AS; 38 (LO), Walter Perkins/SS; 39 (UP), peeterv/iStock; 39 (LO), RichLegg/GI; 40, Jan Holm/Alamy Stock Photo; 40 (inset), SI, NMNH; 41 (UP), Susan E. Degginger/Science Source; 41 (LO), Reri Saputra/SS; 42 (UP), vvoe/AS; 42 (LO), Davide Trolli/SS; 43, Belikova Oksana/SS; 44 (UP LE), Andoni Alvarez/SI, NMNH; 44 (UP RT), vvoe/AS; 44 (LO LE), Andoni Alvarez/SI, NMNH; 44 (LO RT), Kelsey Falquero/SI, NMNH; 45 (UP), sonsart/SS; 45 (LO LE), Vitaliy Balenko/SS; 45 (LO RT), Andoni Alvarez/SI, NMNH; 46 (UP), Goh Chai Hin/AFP/GI; 46 (LO), Walter Perkins/SS; 47, Chris Saulit/GI; 48 (UP), alice_photo/AS; 48 (LO), Raylipscombe/iStock; 48-49, Marcos Souza/DRMS; 50 (UP), Yun Gao/DRMS; 50 (LO), ESB Professional/SS; 51 (UP LE), Irina Schmidt/AS; 51 (UP RT), Belikova Oksana/SS; 51 (CTR LE), Shtraus Dmytro/SS; 51 (CTR RT), alekosa/AS; 51 (LO), Walter Perkins/SS; CHAPTER 3: 52-53, Pixattitude/DRMS; 54-55, Albert Russ/SS, Courtesy of The Metropolitan Museum; 56 (UP), SI, NMNH; 56 (LO), Alexstar/DRMS; 56-57, Clearviewstock/DRMS; 58, Jarcosa/DRMS; 59 (UP), carlosdelacalle/SS; 59 (LO), NataliyaF/SS; 60 (UP), Cristina Romero Palma/SS; 60 (LO), Besedin Igor/SS; 60-61, Konstantin Pukhov/DRMS; 62, Chip Clark/SI; 62 (inset), Chris Ratcliffe/Bloomberg/GI; 63, The Print Collector/Alamy Stock Photo; 64 (UP), Ekaterina Kriminskaya/DRMS; 65, Nevena Marjanovic/SS; 65, Peter Carsten/National Geographic Image Collection; 66 (UP), Björn Wylezich/AS; 66 (LO), Maha Heang 245789/AS; 66-67, ArtushFoto/AS; 67, fotofabrika/AS; 68, Victoria Jones/AFP/GI; 69 (UP), luchschenF/SS; 69 (LO), SS; 70 (UP LE), Chip Clark/SI; 70 (UP CTR), Joel Arem/Science Photo Library; 70 (UP RT), Laurent Gillieron/EPA/SS; 70 (LO LE), Peter Macdiarmid/GI; 70 (LO RT), Dane A. Penland/SI; 71 (LE), mulrooney russia/Alamy Stock Photo; 71 (UP RT), Paul Davey/Barcroft Images/GI; 71 (LO RT), Courtesy of The Metropolitan Museum; 72 (UP), Alexmar/AS; 72 (LO), Sinclair Stammers/Science Photo Library; 72-73, Subbotina Anna/AS; 73, vladk213/AS; 74 (LE), Simon Zenger/DRMS; 74 (UP RT), SI, NMNH; 74 (LO RT), SunChan/GI; 75 (UP), Roy Palmer/SS; 75 (CTR RT), Ruslan Minakryn/DRMS; 75 (LO LE), Sergei Denisov/DRMS; 75 (LO RT), optimarc/SS; 76 (UP), jonnysek/AS; 76 (CTR), Dusan Zidar/SS; 76 (LO), Milan Gonda/SS; 76-77, Eric Broder Van Dyke/DRMS; 78 (UP), Mehmet Gokhan Bayhan/AS; 78 (LO), Joseph Sohm/SS; 79, Leonid Andronov/AS; 80, J. Palys/SS; 81 (UP), Enlightened Media/SS; 81 (LO), Petri jauhiainen/SS; 82 (UP), Björn Wylezich/AS; 82 (LO), bonchan/SS; 83, Mirekdeml/DRMS; 84 (UP A), Canstock Photo; 84 (UP B), Vinicius Tupinamba/AS; 84 (UP C), NickKnight/SS; 84 (UP D), LifetimeStock/SS; 84 (UP E), boykung/SS; 84 (UP F): Vladimir Vydrin/AS; 84 (LO A), Ingemar Magnusson/DRMS; 84 (LO B), imfotograf/AS; 84 (LO C), ArtEvent ET/AS; 84 (LO D), Ekaterina/AS; 84 (LO E), Ilizia/SS; 84 (LO F), bjphotographs/AS; 85 (UP A), Zelfit/DRMS; 85 (UP B), Courtesy of The Metropolitan Museum; 85 (UP C), NickKnight/SS; 85 (UP D), DiamondGalaxy/AS; 85 (UP E), Joel Arem/Science Source; 85 (UP F), sudjai banthaothuk/SS; 85 (LO A), Stellar Gems/SS; 85 (LO B), photoworld/AS; 85 (LO C), Albert Russ/SS; 85 (LO D), Minakryn Ruslan/SS; 85 (LO E), Epitavi/SS; 85 (LO F), Pancaketom/DRMS; CHAPTER 4: 86-87, Natador/DRMS; 88, Kosobu/DRMS; 89 (UP LE), wildestanimal/GI; 89 (UP RT), Avictorero/DRMS; 89 (LO), GI Plus/iStock; 90 (UP), David Acosta Allely/SS; 90 (LO), AlexeyMasliy/iStockphoto/GI; 91 (LE), Romantik89/AS; 91 (RT), Courtesy of The Metropolitan Museum; 92, Alessandrozocc/DRMS; 93 (UP), Mirelle/SS; 93 (LO), Juan de Roux; 94, Daniela Migliorisi/SS; 94-95, Reinhard Dirscherl/GI; 96, WaterFrame/Alamy Stock Photo; 97, Amber Davis; 98-99, Stephen Frink/GI; 100 (UP), Akiyoko74/DRMS.com; 100 (LO), Bayhu19/SS; 101 (UP LE), Gabriel Paladino; 101 (UP RT), nessaflame/iStock; 101 (LO LE), SailingAway/AS; 101 (LO RT), Terios/SS; 102, Harry Rogers/Science Source; 103 (UP), Daniel Wright98/SS; 103 (LO), Bruno Bleu/SS; 104, Nature Picture Library/Alamy Stock Photo; 105 (LE), socrates471/SS; 105 (RT), Andoni Alvarez/SI, NMNH; 106-107, imageBROKER/Alamy Stock Photo; 107, Jenifer DeLemont/SS; 108 (UP), Norman Lopez/iStock; 108 (LO), Comstock Images/GI; 109 (UP LE), Bonnie Taylor Barry/SS; 109 (UP RT), Lori Owenby; 109 (LO LE), Armin Rose/SS; 109 (LO RT), Joop Hoek/AS; 110 (UP), Paul Starosta/GI; 110 (LO), blickwinkel/Alamy Stock Photo; 111 (UP), Historic Collection/Alamy Stock Photo; 111 (LO), murasal/AS; 112 (LE), Danny Iacob/SS; 112 (RT), Natalia van D/SS; 113, diveivanov/AS; 114-115 (UP), murasal/AS; 114-115 (LO), BIOSPHOTO/Alamy Stock Photo; 115, Danita Delimont/Alamy Stock Photo; 116 (LE), Freer/SS; 116 (UP RT), Andoni Alvarez/SI, NMNH; 116 (LO RT), Joy Prescott/AS; 117 (UP LE), mtilghma/iStock; 117 (UP RT), Andoni Alvarez/SI, NMNH; 117 (CTR), Cesare Antonio Palma/DRMS; 117 (LO LE), Andoni Alvarez/SI, NMNH; 117 (LO RT), Andoni Alvarez/SI, NMNH; 118 (UP), SI, NMNH; 118 (CTR), Bayhu19/SS; 118 (LO), Danny Iacob/SS; 119 (UP LE), David Acosta Allely/SS; 119 (UP CTR), Daniela Migliorisi/SS; 119 (CTR RT), Historic Collection/Alamy Stock Photo; 119 (LO), Nature Picture Library/Alamy Stock Photo; 120 (UP), Robbie Shone/National Geographic Image Collection; 120 (CTR LE), Balefire/SS; BACK MATTER: 120 (CTR RT), Florin Burlan/SS; 120 (LO), Shakeyimages/DRMS.com; 121 (UP LE), LuFeeTheBear/SS; 121 (UP RT), Arabes/DRMS; 121 (LO LE), photastic/SS; 121 (LO CTR), Pat_Hastings/SS; 121 (LO RT), Sarah Marchant/SS; 123, Peter Carsten/National Geographic Image Collection; 124 (LE), Virz87/DRMS; 125 (LE), Daniel127001/DRMS; 125 (RT), Eli Maier/SS; 128, Phil Degginger/Science Source

To Bernice and Brenna, my brilliant shelling buddies, with thanks! —M.R.D.

The publisher acknowledges and thanks Steve Tomecek for his expert insight and guidance.
Many thanks also to project manager Grace Hill Smith, researcher Michelle Harris, and
photo editor Sharon Dortenzio for their invaluable help with this book.

Copyright © 2021 National Geographic Partners, LLC

All rights reserved. Reproduction of the whole or any part of the
contents without written permission from the publisher is prohibited.

NATIONAL GEOGRAPHIC and Yellow Border Design are trademarks
of the National Geographic Society, used under license.

Since 1888, the National Geographic Society has funded more than
12,000 research, exploration, and preservation projects around the
world. The Society receives funds from National Geographic Partners,
LLC, funded in part by your purchase. A portion of the proceeds from
this book supports this vital work. To learn more, visit natgeo.com/info.

For more information, visit nationalgeographic.com,
call 1-877-873-6846, or write to the following address:

National Geographic Partners, LLC
1145 17th Street N.W.
Washington, DC 20036-4688 U.S.A.

For librarians and teachers: nationalgeographic.com/books/
librarians-and-educators

More for kids from National Geographic: natgeokids.com

National Geographic Kids magazine inspires children to explore
their world with fun yet educational articles on animals, science,
nature, and more. Using fresh storytelling and amazing photography,
Nat Geo Kids shows kids ages 6 to 14 the fascinating truth about
the world—and why they should care.
kids.nationalgeographic.com/subscribe

For rights or permissions inquiries, please contact
National Geographic Books Subsidiary Rights:
bookrights@natgeo.com

Designed by Eva Absher-Schantz

Hardcover ISBN: 978-1-4263-7222-3
Reinforced library binding ISBN: 978-1-4263-7223-0

Printed in Hong Kong
21/PPHK/1

UNCUT EMERALD